SUPER BOWL SUPERSTARS

PEYTON MANNING
and the
Indianapolis Colts

SUPER BOWL XLI

by Michael Sandler

Consultant: Norries Wilson
Head Football Coach
Columbia University

BEARPORT
PUBLISHING

New York, New York

Credits

Cover and Title Page, © Jed Jacobsohn/Getty Images; 4, © REUTERS/Marc Serota; 5, © Paul Spinelli/Getty Images; 6, © Bill Frakes/Sports Illustrated; 7, Courtesy of The Times-Picayune, New Orleans; 8, © Rick Stewart/Allsport/Getty Images; 9, © Al Pereira/WireImage.com; 10, © REUTERS/Brent Smith; 11, © REUTERS/Scott Olson; 12L, © APImages/Susan Ragan; 12C, © Patrick D. Witty/ Getty Images; 12R, © Bettmann/CORBIS; 13, © Peter Brouillet/WireImage.com; 14, © AP Photo/Elise Amendola; 15, © AP Images/Charles Krupa; 16, © Paul Spinelli/ Getty Images; 17, © Doug Benc/Getty Images; 18, © REUTERS/Shaun Best; 19, © Joe Robbins/Getty Images; 20, © REUTERS/Gary Cameron; 21, © Donald Miralle/ Getty Images; 22L, © AP Images/David J. Phillip; 22R, © Ronald Martinez/Getty Images; 22 Background, © AP Images/Mark Duncan.

Publisher: Kenn Goin
Senior Editor: Lisa Wiseman
Creative Director: Spencer Brinker
Design: Deborah Kaiser
Photo Researcher: Jennifer Bright

Library of Congress Cataloging-in-Publication Data

Sandler, Michael.
 Peyton Manning and the Indianapolis Colts : Super Bowl XLI / by Michael Sandler.
     p. cm. — (Super Bowl superstars)
 Includes bibliographical references and index.
 ISBN-13: 978-1-59716-540-2 (library binding)
 ISBN-10: 1-59716-540-9 (library binding)
 1. Manning, Peyton—Juvenile literature. 2. Football players—United States—
Biography—Juvenile literature. 3. Super Bowl (41st : 2007 : Miami Gardens, FL)—
Juvenile literature. I. Title.

 GV939.M289S26 2008
 796.332092—dc22
 (B)
                           2007007984

For more information, write to Bearport Publishing Company, Inc., 101 Fifth Avenue, Suite 6R, New York, New York 10003. Printed in the United States of America.

10 9 8 7 6 5 4 3

★ Contents ★

Not Again

Peyton Manning held dozens of passing records. He had won countless awards. At the moment, however, these **honors** weren't important. Only one thing mattered to the quarterback—beating the New England Patriots in the 2006–2007 **AFC Championship Game**.

Twice the Patriots had defeated Peyton's Indianapolis Colts on the way to the Super Bowl. Now they were doing it again. New England was ahead by 18 points. Could Peyton stop another painful loss?

Peyton Manning

Peyton leads his team during the 2006–2007 AFC Championship Game.

In both 2003 and 2004, Peyton was named the National Football League's (NFL) Most Valuable Player (MVP).

Football Family

For Peyton, football was a family game. His father, Archie, was a star quarterback in the NFL. His two brothers, Eli and Cooper, liked to play as well. To the Manning kids, picking up a football was as natural as learning to crawl.

Like his dad, Peyton became a talented passer. With Peyton as **starting** quarterback, his high school team won 34 of 39 games. Coaches of **opposing** teams were happy to see him leave for college.

The Mannings (from top left):
Cooper, Peyton, Olivia, Archie, and Eli.

As a high school senior, Peyton was named National Player of the Year.

Peyton's brother Eli is the quarterback for the New York Giants.

College Star

Peyton's powerful arm made him a star at the University of Tennessee. He threw for thousands of yards (meters) and set national passing records.

Peyton didn't just throw a lot. He also threw carefully. Peyton's passes were rarely **intercepted**.

Many NFL teams wanted Peyton to play for them. In 1998, the Indianapolis Colts chose him with the very first pick in the **draft**.

During a game against the Kentucky Wildcats, Peyton passed for 523 yards (478 m).

On draft day, Peyton holds up his Colts jersey.

Peyton finished his college career as the Tennessee Volunteers' all-time leading passer. He set 33 different passing records at the school.

MANNING
18

Turning Around the Colts

The Colts had been one of the NFL's most successful teams. In 1971, when they played in Baltimore, the team had won Super Bowl V (5). The late 1990s, however, had been tough. Indianapolis won just three games each in 1997 and 1998.

Peyton was the spark the team needed. As a **rookie**, he passed for 26 touchdowns. The following year, in 1999, he led the Colts to a **division** title.

Peyton during his rookie season

Peyton throwing a pass during
the first quarter of the playoff
game following the 1999 season

The Colts won ten more
games in 1999 than the
season before—the biggest
turnaround in NFL history!

Almost the Best

As in high school and college, Peyton became the quarterback that coaches hated to face. He was among the best passers that anyone had ever seen. There was only one thing he didn't have—a **Super Bowl ring**. The greatest quarterbacks, such as Joe Namath, Joe Montana, and John Elway, always won the big games. They had their rings to prove it.

After eight NFL seasons, Peyton didn't have one. He had never taken the Colts to the Super Bowl.

Joe Montana

John Elway

Joe Namath

Peyton (#18) hands off the ball to Dominic Rhodes (#33) during a game in 2004.

Peyton holds the NFL record for most touchdown passes in a single season. This record was set in 2004.

The Powerful Patriots

Each year a team came along and knocked the Colts out of the playoffs. Usually it was the New England Patriots and their quarterback Tom Brady.

Peyton had better **statistics**. Tom, however, had the big wins. He was famous for leading last-minute, game-winning **drives**. In both 2004 and 2005, the Patriots beat Indianapolis and went on to win the Super Bowl.

Through 2006, Tom Brady had a 12-1 record in playoff games. He also had three Super Bowl rings.

A disappointed Peyton

A Different Ending

When the Patriots took an 18-point lead in the 2006–2007 AFC Championship Game, another loss for the Colts seemed certain. Then Peyton took over.

Due to his amazing passing, the Colts slowly narrowed the New England lead. With two minutes left, however, the Colts still trailed. Peyton, though, wouldn't be stopped. He picked apart the New England defense on an 80-yard (73-m) touchdown drive. Indianapolis won, 38-34.

Bryan Fletcher catches a key 32-yard (29-m) pass during the AFC Championship Game.

Joseph Addai scores the winning touchdown on the Colts' final drive of the game.

The Colts' AFC victory sent the team into Super Bowl XLI (41). This was the team's first Super Bowl appearance since 1971.

Super Bowl XLI (41)

In Super Bowl XLI (41), Indianapolis was **favored** to beat the Chicago Bears. Within seconds, however, the Colts fell behind.

On the opening kickoff, the Bears' Devin Hester zigzagged 92 yards (84 m) for a touchdown. Bears fans went crazy. The Colts' players looked shocked.

Peyton, though, quickly struck back. He found Reggie Wayne for a 53-yard (48-m) touchdown pass. Then, Chicago scored again, stretching their lead to 14-6.

Devin's (#23) opening kickoff return was the longest in Super Bowl history.

Reggie Wayne scores a
first quarter touchdown
for the Colts.

Beating the Bears

Peyton, however, would not be denied his ring. Again and again, he moved his team downfield. Three drives led to field goals. A fourth ended with a touchdown run by Dominic Rhodes.

On the **defensive** end, the Colts forced five **turnovers**. They held Chicago to only three points in the second half.

At the end of the game, the Colts were the winners. The final score was 29-17. At last—like Montana, Elway, and Namath—Peyton Manning was a Super Bowl champion.

Kelvin Hayden scores the Colts' final touchdown.

Peyton and the Colts' coach,
Tony Dungy, celebrate their
Super Bowl win.

Peyton was named the
MVP of Super Bowl XLI (41).

★ Key Players ★

There were other key players on the Indianapolis Colts who helped win Super Bowl XLI (41). Here are two of them.

★ Kelvin Hayden #26

Position: Cornerback

Born: 7/23/1983 in Chicago, Illinois

Height: 6' 0" (1.83 m)

Weight: 195 pounds (88 kg)

Key Play: Intercepted a pass and ran it back for the Colts' final touchdown

★ Dominic Rhodes #33

Position: Running Back

Born: 1/17/1979 in Waco, Texas

Height: 5' 9" (1.75 m)

Weight: 203 pounds (92 kg)

Key Plays: Ran 21 times for 113 yards (103 m) and 1 touchdown

AFC Championship Game
(AY-EFF-SEE CHAM-pee-uhn-*ship*
GAME) a playoff game that
decides which AFC (American
Football Conference) team will
go to the Super Bowl

defensive (di-FEN-siv)
the part of the game that involves
stopping the other team from
scoring

division (di-VIZH-uhn)
teams that are grouped together
within the AFC (American
Football Conference) or NFC
(National Football Conference)
and compete against each other
for a playoff spot

draft (DRAFT)
an event in which NFL teams
choose college players to be on
their teams

drives (DRIVEZ)
a series of plays that begin when
a team gets the ball; the plays
end when the team with the ball
either scores or gives up the ball
to the other team.

favored (FAY-vurd)
expected to win

honors (ON-urz)
awards

intercepted (*in*-tur-SEP-tid)
had a pass caught by a player
on the other team

opposing (uh-POHZ-ing)
other teams playing against
one's own team

rookie (RUK-ee)
a player who is in his first year of
professional football

starting (START-ing)
playing at the very beginning of
the game; the best player for that
position

statistics (stuh-TISS-tiks)
numbers, such as the amount of
touchdowns or passes completed,
that show how well a player does

Super Bowl ring (SOO-pur BOHL
RING) a ring given to each
player on the team that wins
the Super Bowl

turnovers (TURN-*oh*-vurz)
plays that result in the loss of
the football to the other team

Bibliography

The New York Times

sportsillustrated.cnn.com

www.colts.com

www.indystar.com

Read More

Horn, Geoffrey M. *Peyton Manning.* Milwaukee, WI: Gareth Stevens Publishing (2005).

Mattern, Joanne. *Peyton Manning: Indianapolis Colts Star Quarterback.* Hockessin, DE: Mitchell Lane Publishers (2006).

Stewart, Mark. *The Indianapolis Colts.* Chicago, IL: Norwood House Press (2006).

Learn More Online

To learn more about Peyton Manning, the Indianapolis Colts, and the Super Bowl, visit **www.bearportpublishing.com/SuperBowlSuperstars**

Index